WE ARE AN
EASTER PEOPLE

The Triumph of God's Love in Our Lives

A Group Process

John and Adrienne Carr

UPPER
ROOM BOOKS®
NASHVILLE

Contents

A Letter to Participants

Dear Friends:

What is it about Easter that makes it such a special day? What prompts us to turn out for worship in record numbers, all dolled up in our finest clothes? Certainly the promise of spring with its warmth and blossoming new life is worth celebrating, but the timing isn't always right, and the weather is as likely to be shivery as it is to be sunny. There obviously is more to it. Is it the message that because Jesus was raised from the dead we too can hope for life beyond the grave for ourselves and those we love? That's got to be an important part of it.

But that still is not the whole story. Easter is not just about a resurrection from physical death. It is about the triumph of God's love for us over *everything* that threatens to rob our lives of meaning and joy. It is about the power to live *this* life victoriously, a power which turns . . .

strangers into gifts,
wounded people into healers,
self-centered people into servants,
victims into victors,
and people who seem to have very little into wealthy investors.

Experiencing more of that power and learning how we can tap into it more often is what *We Are an Easter People* is all about. We developed the process with the help of several hundred courageous souls in over twenty churches who tried it out in its earliest forms and gave us countless valuable suggestions. Their word is, "It works!" Our hope is that through it you too will discover afresh that . . .

Christ is risen indeed!

Adrienne and John Carr

5

1

Gifted Strangers

Exploring Our Gifts and Hopes

We are "gifted strangers." In connection with each of our sessions, we will be thinking about some aspects about ourselves which might be gifts to others in the Christian community. To start with, let's each look at (and jot down) some of our specific skills, knowledge, and talents in the following categories:

Arts and Crafts

House and Garden

Hobbies

Languages I Know

Other Places/Countries I've Traveled or Lived In

Now, think about and write down your responses to these two things:

1. A gift you have that you are willing to tell the rest of the group about, either a particularly strong gift or (more fun) one which you are pretty sure they wouldn't suspect!

Patience - Erick

Courage - Sharon

2. One hope you have for what this program might mean to you.

Erick - Gain knowledge, Get caught up in work/life to enjoy snow/work on house

Sharon - Career hopes

My Group's Gifts and Hopes

Name   Gift   Hope

_____

_____

_____

_____

_____

_____

_____

_____

_____

_____

_____

_____

_____

_____

2

Wounded Healers

1. Take time to see each person in your group (including yourself!) "real" each day. A helpful way to do this is to try first to picture the person who goes with the name (this first week you may not be able to do that), remember anything you can which he or she said in the session, and look at your list to see what gift and hope he or she shared. Maybe there is a way in which you can affirm that gift or help the hope to be realized. Think about how God accepts and loves this person without reservations. Then go on to the next person. When you've finished ponder this poem:

Persons Are Gifts

at least Jesus thought so: "Father, I want those you have given me to be where I am . . ."

   I agree with Jesus . . . and I also want those whom the Father has given to me to be where I am.

Persons are gifts which the Father sends to me wrapped!

   Some are wrapped very beautifully; they are very attractive when I first see them.
   Some come in very ordinary wrapping paper.
   Once in a while there is a "Special delivery"!!
   Some persons are gifts which come very loosely wrapped; others very tightly.

But the wrapping is not the gift:

> It is so easy to make this mistake . . . it's amusing when babies do it.
> Sometimes the gift is very easy to open up.
> Sometimes I need others to help.
>
> > Is it because they are afraid? Does it hurt?
> > Maybe they have been opened up before and thrown away!
> > Could it be that the gift is not for me?

I am a person. Therefore, I am a gift too!

> A gift to myself, first of all. The Father gave myself to me.
> Have I ever really looked inside the wrappings? Afraid to?
> Perhaps I've never accepted the gift that I am . . .
> Could it be that there is something else inside the wrappings than what
> I think there is?
>
> Maybe I've never seen the wonderful gift that I am?
> Could the Father's gifts be anything but beautiful?
> I love the gifts which those who love me give me; why not this gift from
> the Father?

And I am a gift to other persons.

> Am I willing to be given by the Father to others? . . .
> a person for others!
> Do others have to be content with the wrappings . . .
> never permitted to enjoy the gift?

Every meeting of persons is an exchange of gifts.

> But a gift without a giver is not a gift;
> it is a thing devoid of a relationship to a giver or givee.

Friendship is a relationship between persons who see themselves as they
truly are:

> gifts of the Father to each other for others . . .

BROTHERS AND SISTERS!

A friend is a gift not just to me but to others through me . . .

> When I keep my friend—possess him or her—I destroy their "giftness."
> If I save her or his life for me, I lose it; if I lose it for others, I save it.

12

Session 2

Persons are gifts, gifts received and gifts given . . . like the Son.

Friendship is the response of persons—gifts to the Father-Giver. Friendship is

EUCHARIST!

—Peggy Ferrell

2. Meet with your partner for this week. You might want to talk more about the gifts you listed for yourselves.

3. Read and reflect on the following at least a couple of times during the week:

A Company of Strangers, Yet the Body of Christ

In the first session we looked at how Easter can take us, a diverse bunch of lonely people, strangers to one another, and make us the body of Christ, a community which makes the love of God visible and believable, not only to us but also to the world around us.

What is it that makes this happen? It's the good news, to begin with, that Christ died for all of us. It's the news that God loves those strangers around us with the same unconditional love God gives to us. Secondly, it is the gift of the spirit of this same Christ who now lives and moves among us, drawing us together as a deeply supportive and freeing fellowship, seeking to use us as Christ's body.

But the message won't make much difference if we don't apply it in the way we look at one another, if we fail to make the effort to see each other real. And the Spirit never forces itself upon us. We have to be willing to be open to it.

The Key: Hospitality

One word above all others in the Christian tradition suggests the quality of caring which lets the Spirit turn strangers into gifts. It is the

13

word *hospitality*. We know from experience what real hospitality feels like. It means being received openly, warmly, without the need to earn your keep or prove yourself. An inhospitable space is one in which we feel invisible—or visible, but on trial. A hospitable space is alive with trust and goodwill, rooted in a sense of our common humanity. When we enter such a space we feel valued, because the host assumes we are. Here there are no preconceptions about how we "should" or "must" be. Here we are accepted for who and what we are. Hospitality means letting the stranger remain a stranger while offering acceptance nonetheless. It means meeting the stranger's needs while allowing him or her to simply be, without attempting to make him or her over into a modified version of ourselves.

Hospitality means inviting the stranger into our private space, whether that be the space of our own home or the space of our personal awareness and concern. And when we do, some important transformations occur. Our private space is suddenly enlarged; no longer as tight and cramped and restricted but open and expansive and free. And our space may also be illumined. Who knows how the presence of the stranger may throw light on some aspect of our lives which we had not seen before—a bias, a misapprehension, a hidden treasure, a gift? Through the stranger our view of ourselves, of our world, and of God is deepened and expanded. Through the stranger we are given a chance to find ourselves. And through the stranger God finds us and offers us the gift of wholeness in the midst of our estranged and lonely lives.

A Problem: Finding the Right Stranger

However, even when we consider the benefits of hospitality, it is hard to think of ourselves welcoming just any strangers into our private space, especially needy strangers. We usually select our guests carefully, inviting people whom we enjoy, whom we warm up to easily, who call forth our love. The problem is: most of the people around us do not awaken those sorts of feelings in us.

This seems to be the problem of a certain lawyer who decided to put Jesus on the spot:

And behold, a lawyer stood up to put him to the test, saying, "Teacher, what shall I do to inherit eternal life?" He said to him, "What is written in the law? How do you read?" And he answered, "You shall love the Lord your God with all your heart, and with all your soul, and with all your

14

strength, and with all your mind; and your neighbor as yourself." And he said to him, "You have answered right; do this, and you will live."

But he, desiring to justify himself, said to Jesus, "and who is my neighbor?"

—Luke 10:25-29

This is the question which causes Jesus to tell the most famous story of hospitality in the Bible, the parable of the good Samaritan. Note that the lawyer is not asking Jesus to tell him *how* to love his neighbors. He asks: *Who* is my neighbor? Whom should I love? Where can I find someone—anyone—who has proven or will prove to be such a neighbor to me that he or she calls forth my unconditional love? Actually, he might have gone on to say: I don't really love myself very well. In fact, the very things about my neighbors which make it hardest for me to love them are the things which mirror my own needs and fears, my own unloveliness.

The lawyer is asking, then, about where you get the power to love *all* of your neighbors and, yes, *all* of yourself!

Jesus' Answer

Keep this question in mind as you read the familiar story which follows. Remember too these important facts about the characters:

The priest probably was returning home after serving his two-week stint of service in the Temple at Jerusalem. Priesthood was a hereditary job, and it involved some interesting taboos. A priest could not touch a corpse. It was believed that doing so would render him unworthy and unable to deal with sacred things, and he would have to undergo an elaborate ritual cleansing in order to go back to work.

Levites were lay associates who helped the priests run the vast Temple operation. They probably handled religious education and ongoing administration, while the rotating priests led worship.

Samaritans were an ethnic minority living in their own territory between Galilee and Judea. They were descendants of people imported to resettle the area after hated Assyria had devastated the northern kingdom of Israel and exiled her people to faraway parts of its empire seven hundred years before. As such, they were a continual reminder of that tragic and humiliating defeat. To make matters worse, they had developed their own version of Judaism and had built a rival temple of their own. Jews didn't just dislike the Samaritans, they hated them. Here's the story:

A man was going down from Jerusalem to Jericho, and he fell among robbers, who stripped him and beat him, and departed, leaving him half dead. Now by chance a priest was going down that road; and when he saw him he passed by on the other side. So likewise a Levite, when he came to the place and saw him, passed by on the other side. But a Samaritan, as he journeyed, came to where he was; and when he saw him, he had compassion, and went to him and bound up his wounds, pouring on oil and wine; then he set him on his own beast and brought him to an inn, and took care of him. And the next day he took out two denarii and gave them to the innkeeper, saying, "Take care of him; and whatever more you spend, I will repay you when I come back." Which of these three, do you think, proved neighbor to the man who fell among the robbers?

—Luke 10:30-36

A question to think about:

What do you think Jesus is saying here about where you and I can get the power to love our neighbors and *all* of ourselves?

3

Chosen Ministers

1. Take time each day to think about every member of your group. If you've been using the list you made in Session One, try starting at different points on it. Think about what each person said over the meal about their coming week. Remember the wounds of those you shared with in the smaller group. Think of your own wound and of Christ going to whatever lengths are necessary to heal you.

2. Meet with your partner for this week. We suggest that you read the pages in this section and fill out the "gift list" before you do. Then you might share whatever you would like from the list with her or him.

3. Read the following, think about the questions it poses, and fill out the "gift list."

The Wounded Healer

In his book *The Wounded Healer*, Henri J. M. Nouwen repeats an old Jewish legend.

Rabbi Yoshua ben Levi came upon Elijah the prophet while he was standing by the entrance to Rabbi Simeron ben Yohai's cave . . . He asked Elijah, "When will the Messiah come?" Elijah replied,
"Go and ask him yourself."
"Where is he?"
"Sitting at the gates of the city."
"How shall I know him?"
"He is sitting among the poor covered with wounds. The others unbind all their wounds at the same time and then bind them up again. But he

17

unbinds one at a time and binds it up again, saying to himself, 'Perhaps I shall be needed: if so I must always be ready so as not to delay for a moment.' "

The story suggests that, because he binds his own wounds one at a time, the Messiah would not have to take time to prepare himself if asked to help someone else. He would be ready to help.

Jesus has given this story a new fullness by making his own broken body the way to health and new life. Not only did he care for his own wounds and the wounds of others, he made his wounds into a major source of his healing power. Moreover, through his body, the Christian community, he makes it possible for us to do the same.

But it cannot happen unless we are willing to go through the sometimes scary and painful process of sharing our pain with one another. Our culture places such a premium on being "all together" that we tend to draw back from admitting our brokenness, sometimes even to ourselves. Yet when we do, our wounds cease to paralyze and separate us. They bring us into a deep fellowship with one another as needy human beings. They open us to the amazing grace of Christ, the good Samaritan. And they empower us to begin to use our experiences of suffering in the service of others.

The big point of Session One was that our differences, our uniqueness, can make us surprising gifts to one another. The message of Session Two is that our sufferings can as well.

Consider your own wounds:

Which ones do you still hide or hug to yourself?

Where might you go in the Christian community to "bind them up"?

Session 3

What out of your own painful experiences might make you especially qualified to reach out with healing hospitality to another person going through something similar?

Think about the life experiences you've gone through which might be gifts to others. Here are some categories to help you think about them. This is your own private list. What, if anything, you want to share of it will be entirely up to you.

Gifts Growing Out of My Own Life Experiences

Loss (Death, Divorce)

Career Change (Job Loss, Job Change, Moving)

Coping with Relatives (Family You Grew Up in or Present Family)

Preschoolers (could include daycare, special problems, travel or moving with)

Children

Adolescents

Aging parents

Coping with Medical Problems (could be a problem you have had yourself or one which someone close to you has had)

Particular illnesses or handicaps

Alcoholism

Drug abuse

Managing Finances

Dealing with Debt

Dealing with Retirement

Financial Planning

Chosen Ministers

All of which brings us to the third remarkable transformation which the risen Christ worked in the lives of the first Easter people. Christ turned self-centered people who had looked at service to others as something to be done after they had taken care of their own needs into persons who felt called to see their whole lives in terms of ministry to their neighbors.

Unfortunately, there are two huge misconceptions of the word *minister* today. First, there is the idea that ministers are a set-apart group of professionals who are to be distinguished from the mass of second-class Christians who do not have the blessing or the burden of being "called." The New Testament knows nothing about such a special class! In the early church all Christians were "clergy," "called" to share in a common ministry. Set-apart professional pastors emerged in church history as a way of helping all Christians fulfill that common ministry.

A church letterhead typically reads:

Jackson Presbyterian Church
Minister: Jane Doaks
Associate Minister: Joe Sloan

It might better read:

Jackson Presbyterian Church
Ministers: All the church members
Assistants to the Ministers: Jane Doaks and Joe Sloan

A second misconception is that ministry only means preacher-type activities such as preaching, teaching, visiting the sick and shut-ins, and the like. *In the New Testament, ministry simply means Christlike service, embodying God's love in everything we are and do in every area of our lives, whether that be plumbing, parenting, or politics.*

Some Words from the Risen Christ about What Ministry's All about

Let's take a closer look at the nature of our ministry, using as our guide the very last appearance of the risen Christ to Peter, as recorded in chapter 21 of the Gospel of John.

Peter, in the Gospels, is not only the leader of the disciples; he is also a representative figure, one who seems to hold up a mirror to all of us in our struggles to follow Christ. For example, after all the fantastic events of Holy Week—Jesus' grand entrance on Palm Sunday, his dramatic clashes with the authorities, his arrest and trial and crucifixion, his amazing resurrection—where does our story find Peter? Back fishing! "Christ is risen! I'm going fishing." Isn't that the story of our lives? After all is said and done, after all the magnificent worship services, exciting and nourishing fellowship, mountaintop experiences, all of us have to return to what we sadly call "the real world," to Monday morning.

What makes this little story so special is that the risen Christ appears to Peter and the others in the middle of the Monday morning world. And after actually helping them with their fishing and sharing breakfast on the beach, Christ gives Peter what one might call a final examination for ministry.

22

When they had finished breakfast, Jesus said to Simon Peter, "Simon, son of John, do you love me more than these?" He said to him, "Yes, Lord; you know that I love you." He said to him, "Feed my lambs." A second time he said to him, "Simon, son of John, do you love me?" He said to him, "Yes, Lord; you know that I love you." He said to him, "Tend my sheep." He said to him the third time, "Simon, son of John, do you love me?" Peter was grieved because he said to him the third time, "Do you love me?" And he said to him, "Lord, you know everything; you know that I love you." Jesus said to him, "Feed my sheep."

—John 21:15-17

If this is a final exam to determine Peter's qualifications for ministry, it is fascinating to note what Christ does *not* ask Peter. Christ does not ask him about what he believes or knows. Christ does not say, "Peter, please outline what you believe about the incarnation, the atonement, and the trinity, and compare and contrast that with the views of two prominent contemporary theologians." Nor does Christ quiz Peter about how obedient he has been. Christ does not say, "Peter, let's take a look at your moral balance sheet."

No, Christ simply asks Peter, three times, whether he *loves* Christ or not. Three times, once for each time Peter had denied ever having known Jesus in the high priest's garden. The basic qualification for ministry is our grateful response to God's freeing and forgiving love made plain in Christ. Nothing else! The real question to be asked of us as Christian disciples is whether or not we really care about Christ and what Christ stands for.

And the instructions about what we are to do if we love Christ are pretty simple as well: "Feed my sheep." We should remember that Christ's sheep, God's sheep, the objects of God's love are not just church members. That famous verse so many of us memorized in Sunday school, John 3:16, reads, "For God so loved the *world* that he gave his only Son . . ." (italics added) and not "God so loved the church. . . ."

If ministry means feeding Christ's sheep, what are some of the biggest hungers or needs to be fed which you can see around you:

in your neighborhood?

at work?

in your city?

in our nation?

elsewhere in the world?

Which ones especially move you?

4

Victorious Victims

1. Take time to see each person in your group real each day. Think about what he or she shared last time. You might ask yourself, *How might I make the love of God more believable to* _____?

2. Review the parish list you made. Now that you have the time to think more carefully about it, are there names you would want to add? to subtract? Which people on that list should you really try to see real every day? Try it! And also try doing the same for a rotating group of two or three others. You will be surprised at the difference it can make.

3. Meet with your partner for this week. You might talk about your response to the prayer walk in the last session, your reactions to the reading below, and some of the gifts for ministry which you identify from the reading.

4. Read the following:

Concern for the World in Which We Are Called to Minister

We hope you found the prayer walk in your last session to be a touching experience, that it moved you to think more about how you can do more to reach out to make God's love believable. But we also have a hunch that it may have evoked another feeling too, a sense of being overwhelmed by the need and pain around us in our world. Actually we don't need a special prayer walk to produce such a feeling. All kinds of daily incidents can trigger it.

Take a moment to take a couple of deep breaths, relax, and let two or three things come to mind that made you concerned for our world this past week. Maybe it was a story in the paper or something you saw on television, an article, or something someone told you about. Whatever it was that triggered your concern, think about what you pictured in your mind, what feelings and thoughts you had.

Incidents and images may have surfaced for you immediately. Or, you may have found it hard to think of something, while at the same time feeling a growing sense of discomfort—even dread. Whatever your response to this exercise, you are not alone. Though our styles of response may differ, we are all citizens of the same planet, all trying in different ways to cope with a deep, common sense of peril.

The danger comes from three sources. Each of them is a development of unprecedented and catastrophic proportion. Each seems to be growing almost daily in intensity. And each is a standard feature of our awareness of the world.

The Threat of Nuclear War

Much of our government's power and policy is based on the credibility of this threat. Both large and small nations have poured, and continue to pour, trillions of dollars into the proliferation of weapons capable of destroying life on our planet countless times over. And nothing in history suggests that these weapons won't be used or unleashed by accident. Our awareness of this fact is so potent and pervasive that, according to polls, the majority of the public expects a nuclear war to occur within their lifetimes, that they will not survive it, and that civilization as we know it will end.

The Progressive Destruction of Our Life-Support System

Toxic wastes, acid rain, oil spills, rising rates of radioactivity, the erosion of the ozone layer, the destruction of forests, spreading deserts—these facts assail us through news reports and our own experience of the air we breathe, the water we drink, and what we see happening to the environment with our own eyes. And with population and consumption and production growing, it is difficult to see how we can avoid even larger-scale disasters.

The Growing Misery of Half the Earth's People

Perhaps the greatest irony of our day and age is that for all of the so-called progress of our time, never before in history has so large a proportion of humanity lacked the means for a decent and healthy life.

Session 4

The gap between haves and have-nots widens. Massive, public suffering inflicted by human beings dwarfs the pain caused by occasional natural disasters. The majority of our fellow human beings live as victims. And the potential destructiveness of their rage makes our planet a tinderbox.

Pain for the World

These are facts of life today. Whatever policies we advocate for dealing with them, they are part of the story we are living now together. To be aware of them at any level is to feel pain for our world and our collective future.

The pain is a compound of many feelings. There is fear—dread of what is overtaking our common life and what may be in store, not just for us but for our loved ones. There is anger, even rage, that we must live our lives under threats that would seem to be avoidable yet keep on growing. There is frustration that we don't seem to be able to do much about it. There is guilt too, for we feel implicated and haunted by the thought that we should be able to avert it. And through it all, there is sorrow, a deep sadness for all that is being lost, for the possibility the whole human enterprise may simply end.

Repression

Nobody is exempt from this pain. To be alive, to be aware, to care even a little means feeling it in our bones. And like impulses of pain in the human body, or in any organism, these impulses serve a positive purpose. They are warning signals.

Yet we tend to repress them, to block them out, to avoid exploring and expressing them. Why? Here are some reasons which one group came up with:

- People would see me as a doomsday, cartoon figure.
- I don't want to depress family and friends.
- I don't want to depress myself.
- I want my kids to be happy. I'm afraid to share my fears with them.
- I don't want to get into an argument about questions so complex and huge that nobody really knows the answers.
- It takes too much time and energy.

- It's too overwhelming to talk about.
- I don't want to appear weak or emotional.
- What good does it do? Why talk about it when there is nothing you can do about it?

Are any of these answers familiar? What reasons could you add to the list?

The Effects of Repression

In her book, *Despair and Personal Power in the Nuclear Age,* Joanna Rogers Macy makes a chilling analysis of the price we pay for blocking out the hurt we feel.

To begin with, this repression fragments our lives and distances us from others, especially those close to us. While on the surface we proceed with business as usual, underneath there is awareness of impending doom. And by our reluctance to talk about it we distance ourselves from each other as do the family and friends of the terminally ill.

To the extent we repress painful feelings about our world, we also tend to screen out the data that provoke them. We become less willing to learn about what is really going on, to process any more news about the perils we face, and what is most dangerous, to press for truly accurate information.

But the bottom line is a sense of powerlessness, futility, apathy. We see ourselves as the victims of forces about which we can do little if anything.

Is Macy's analysis at all on target for you? If so, what effects can you identify in your own life? in the lives of those around you?

A Crisis of Faith

And where is a loving God in all this? Macy suggests that one of the deepest reasons we tend to repress the world's suffering is that we are not sure our faith can face and deal with it, that we possibly can find God in the midst of such darkness.

It is precisely this fear, this question, this longing that the Easter message addresses. For to the disciples, the crucifixion represented the final chilling word about what good people can do. The violent forces which really determine what happens in our world had crushed Jesus and all he stood for. And God hadn't done a thing about it. God's spirit, which had seemed to be operating with power through Jesus' ministry, was nowhere to be seen on Golgotha. The disciples had thought for a while they were going to share in the shaping of history. But now they were back to being victims. It is to these victims that Easter happens.

In the next session we are going to be looking at how the risen Christ dealt with their despair and sense of powerlessness, hoping that in the process we might encounter Christ dealing with our own. We will be using as our guide this classic story of the two disciples on the road to Emmaus. As you read it over, look carefully at the way the risen Christ brings them, step by step, to an awareness of Christ's presence. See if you can identify the steps in the strategy Christ uses to bring them from despair to joyful faith.

That very day two of them were going to a village named Emmaus, about seven miles from Jerusalem, and talking with each other about all these things that had happened. While they were talking and discussing together, Jesus himself drew near and went with them. But their eyes were kept from recognizing him. And he said to them, "What is this conversation which you are holding with each other as you walk?" And they stood still, looking sad. Then one of them, named Cleopas, answered him, "Are you the only visitor to Jerusalem who does not know the things that have happened there in these days?" And he said to them, "What things?" And they said to him, "Concerning Jesus of Nazareth, who was a prophet mighty in deed and word before God and all the people, and how our chief priests and rulers delivered him up to be condemned to death, and crucified him. But we had hoped that he was the one to redeem Israel. Yes, and besides all this, it is now the third day since this happened. Moreover, some women of our company amazed us. They were at the tomb early in the morning and did not find his body; and they came back saying that they had even seen a vision of angels, who said that he was alive. Some of those who were with us went to the tomb, and found it just as the women had said; but him they did not see." And he said to them, "O foolish men and slow of heart to believe all that the prophets have spoken! Was it not necessary that the Christ should suffer these things and enter into his glory?" And beginning with Moses and all the prophets, he interpreted to them in all the scriptures the things concerning himself.

So they drew near to the village to which they were going. He appeared to be going further, but they constrained him, saying, "Stay with us, for it is toward evening and the day is now far spent." So he went in to stay with them. When he was at table with them, he took the bread and blessed, and broke it, and gave it to them. And their eyes were opened and they recognized him; and he vanished out of their sight. They said to each other, "Did not our hearts burn within us while he talked to us on the road, while he opened to us the scriptures?" And they rose that same hour and returned to Jerusalem; and they found the eleven gathered together and those who were with them, who said, "The Lord has risen indeed, and has appeared to Simon!" Then they told what had happened on the road, and how he was known to them in the breaking of the bread.

—Luke 24:13-35

5

Wealthy Investors

The Easter Faith

> Who can separate us from the love of Christ? Can trouble, pain or persecution? Can lack of clothes and food, danger to life and limb, the threat of force of arms? . . .
>
> No, in all these things we win an overwhelming victory through him who has proved his love for us.
>
> I have become absolutely convinced that neither death nor life, neither messenger of Heaven nor monarch of earth, neither what happens today nor what may happen tomorrow, neither a power from on high nor a power from below, nor anything else in God's whole world has any power to separate us from the love of God in Jesus Christ our Lord!
>
> —Romans 8:35, 37-39, PHILLIPS

This is perhaps the most moving and clear statement of the faith of the community to which Easter gave birth. The worst the world's powers could hand out had not been able to defeat Jesus Christ. On the contrary, God had made the cross on which they nailed him the final revelation of God's love. The perils and threats of life were still very real. But Christ had taken away their power to dominate human lives, to rob them of freedom and meaning and joy. The first Christians renounced the authority of the things which ordinarily control and limit our lives. They witnessed to another authority, another power—the lordship of Jesus Christ and the power of the Holy Spirit.

This secret power could not hurt anyone. Nor could it protect a person from suffering. It did not seek to dominate or control others. In fact, it made itself vulnerable to others, opening itself to even more pain at their hands. In short, this power could do none of the things which we usually associate with the word *power*.

But consider what we've been exploring about what it *could* do, what it *did* do, what it *is still doing* in and through the community it created:

31

- The spirit of Christ can take a collection of diverse, basically self-centered human beings and make them a gifted fellowship of people who care about each other and the world (and even themselves!).
- It can set them on fire to fight to change the things in our world which dehumanize and deprive people.
- And, it can empower them to hang in there when everybody else has given up.

Power for a Task

We've been in search of a fresh vision and experience of that power in these last weeks together. And hopefully we have tasted at least something of what that Easter faith is all about. The question now is: Where do we go from here? What difference will it make?

This wasn't at all clear to those who first experienced the presence of the risen Christ. Was God about to bring in the kingdom? Was human history as they knew it about to come to an end and the rule of God's love revealed for all to see forever? They waited and worshiped and wrestled with these questions. And nothing happened. What they began to hear the risen Christ saying to them about the situation is recorded in the first chapter of the Acts of the Apostles:

> *Jesus said:* "It is not for you to know times or seasons which the Father has fixed by his own authority. But you shall receive power when the Holy Spirit has come upon you; and you shall be my witnesses in Jerusalem and in all Judea and Samaria and to the end of the earth."
>
> —Acts 1:7-8

Two big words stand out—*power* and *witnesses:*

1. If the disciples thought what they had experienced together was powerful, they had another thing coming! The gift of even greater *power* was on the way.
2. But that power was *a gift for a task*. It would come to them when, and only when, they caught a vision of their mission as an Easter people: to be Christ's *witnesses*. God was counting on them to make God's love known and believable to all humankind.

We are particularly struck by *where* Christ tells them they are to witness:

- in Jerusalem—among the hometown folks, in their own backyard, so to speak;
- in all Judea—throughout their own nation;
  (Up to this point, the task, though big, seems reasonable. It's only natural for us to feel some responsibility for those who are our "own kind" or "fellow citizens," though that word *all* before Judea might have been a little disconcerting. Then, however, Christ really begins to get unreasonable.)
- in Samaria—among the strange, the different, the outcasts, the heretics, and enemies, the very people about whom they found it most difficult to care;
- and to the ends of the earth—to masses of unknown foreign strangers, seemingly far beyond their reach, and to world problems seemingly far too big for them to even make a dent in.

We believe that this still is Christ's agenda for Christ's people. And that the Spirit comes with real power *only when we are willing to take all of it on.*

After all, when it comes to caring about Jerusalem and much of Judea, we can count on normal human affection, on natural sympathy, even on enlightened self-interest to provide motivation. It's usually when we begin to try to make God's love believable in *all* Judea, in Samaria, and beyond that we really need help from beyond ourselves. And when we need it, when we are willing to acknowledge our inability to meet the challenge on our own, when we are willing to open ourselves to God's power, we get it!

If we don't experience much of the Spirit, it just might be that we have not done the kind of investing of ourselves in God's mission which stretches us beyond our own capacity. Or, it just might be that having faced the challenge, we have tried to tackle it on our own, not looking to God or one another for empowering help.

The Dynamics of Investing

Shortly before his death, Jesus told a parable about our participation in God's mission and its consequences. We're going to use it as the basis for our last exploration as an Easter people, a look at how we are doing and how we hope to do as "Wealthy Investors"!

As they heard these things, he proceeded to tell a parable, because he was near to Jerusalem, and because they supposed that the kingdom of

God was to appear immediately. He said therefore, "A nobleman went into a far country to receive a kingdom and then return. Calling ten of his servants, he gave them ten pounds, and said to them, 'Trade with these till I come.' But his citizens hated him and sent an embassy after him, saying, 'We do not want this man to reign over us.' When he returned, having received the kingdom, he commanded these servants, to whom he had given the money, to be called to him, that he might know what they had gained by trading. The first came before him, saying, 'Lord, your pound has made ten pounds more.' And he said to him, 'Well done, good servant! Because you have been faithful in a very little, you shall have authority over ten cities.' And the second came, saying, 'Lord, your pound has made five pounds.' And he said to him, 'And you are to be over five cities.' Then another came, saying, 'Lord, here is your pound, which I kept laid away in a napkin; for I was afraid of you, because you are a severe man; you take up what you did not lay down, and reap what you did not sow.' He said to him, 'I will condemn you out of your own mouth, you wicked servant! You knew that I was a severe man, taking up what I did not lay down and reaping what I did not sow? Why then did you not put my money into the bank, and at my coming I should have collected it with interest?' And he said to those who stood by, 'Take the pound from him, and give it to him who has the ten pounds.' (And they said to him, 'Lord, he has ten pounds!') 'I tell you, that to every one who has will more be given; but from him who has not, even what he has will be taken away. But as for these enemies of mine, who did not want me to reign over them, bring them here and slay them before me.'"

—Luke 19:11-27

Scholars tell us that the strange verses about the citizens hating the nobleman and about their being rewarded by being slain are probably a reflection of events which happened later and not a part of the original parable. Otherwise the story is pretty straightforward. As Christ's disciples we are an investment society. And God has entrusted to each of us the same operating capital.

But what is the pound? In the currency of that day it amounted to three months wages for an ordinary laborer. But what is its meaning in spiritual terms? This might be an easier question to answer if the boss had given a different amount to each servant. Then we could say that Jesus was talking about intelligence or strength or beauty or position or wealth. And in fact, Jesus did tell another parable in which this is precisely what happens—the parable of the talents in Matthew 25. Here, however, it's different. Everybody gets the very same stake.

The pound, therefore, has to be something which every one of us has been given as a Christian—regardless of age, social standing, job, reputation, looks, health, knowledge, or piety. Only one thing, it seems to us, fits that description. It is something of which we are reminded every time we gather as an Easter people. It is the amazing secret that God loves this wayward, fearful, anxious world unconditionally and even now is at work undercover to transform it.

And what are we to do with this news, this operating capital? The boss gives the same simple instructions to all his servants: "Trade with it until I come." We are to invest the news of God's love for the world in the way we live each day. We are to let that secret govern the way we look at and respond to every person and situation in our lives. For example, that is exactly what we have been trying to do with each other in "seeing each other real" each day.

If that is what Jesus is referring to, then in the rest of the story . . .

- What do you think he is saying about what's in it for us if we follow instructions?
- What do you think he is saying about the consequences of not doing so?
- Why do you suppose the third servant didn't follow through? Can you draw any possible reasons from your own experience?
- Why do you suppose the other two obeyed?

A Look at Your Investment Portfolio and Performance

On the next two pages is a chart which we hope will help you explore and evaluate what you are presently doing in the way of investing God's love and how you feel about it. We urge you to give some quality time to filling it in, trying to be completely honest with yourself in doing so. Nobody but you will see it. What we hope is that it will enable you to identify some of the things that you need help with right now in trying to live the Christian life. Then in the upcoming session you'll have a chance to consult with some other members about how some of those needs might get met. Please follow these steps:

Step One
Work with the chart itself. Again, remember this is not for anyone else's viewing. You can use your own personal shorthand.

Step Two
Look over what you've written and ask yourself: *What do I need right now in my investment program as a Christian disciple?* Most of us proba-

bly have all kinds of needs, different ones in relationship to different parts of the chart. Make a list, trying to be as specific as you can. Here are just a few of the possible items, born of our own experience:

- forgiveness and a fresh start
- encouragement and empowerment
- bigger opportunities (I'm underinvested)
- aid in sorting out what responsible investing means in this area or overall (One can't do everything and can count on the body of Christ to be doing some other things, but how do you decide what is your share?)
- more support (I'm overextended and alone)
- help in cutting my losses

Step Three
Select at least three things in order of importance that you would like some consultation about.

Seeing Each Other Real and Meeting with Your Partner

The first should take on added meaning in light of the above, and the second may give you a chance to talk about some of the things you thought and felt as you reviewed the state of your investments!

Session 5

My Parish

_____ _____

_____ _____

_____ _____

_____ _____

_____ _____

_____ _____

_____ _____

_____ _____

_____ _____

_____ _____

_____ _____

_____ _____

_____ _____

_____ _____

_____ _____

My Investment in Making the Love of God Known and Believable in . . .

Jerusalem	All Judea	Samaria	The Ends of the Earth

Hometown folks:
1. me
2. my family
3. friends
4. colleagues
5. neighbors
6. church
7. my town or city
   and . . .
	My nation:
	1. justice
	2. reconciliation
	3. quality of life
	4. our environment
	5. peace
	6. poverty
	   and . . .
		The enemies of:
		1. our country
		2. our way of life
		3. our prosperity
		4. human rights
		5. the world's stability and
		   survival and . . .
			Global:
			1. hunger
			2. poverty
			3. conflicts
			4. oppression
			5. gaps between haves and
			   have-nots and . . .

How and to what extent are you already investing in the above areas? Describe below. Use numbers to match the items in the boxes above to your comments below.

where you are truly happy with what you are doing, a [-] where you are unhappy, and a [?] where you are not sure. Then comment below.

How do you think God feels about what you've done with the "pound" in each of these areas? Where do you hear God calling you to change, to make a new investment?

John Carr is Professor Emeritus of Church Ministries at Candler School of Theology, Emory University, Atlanta, Georgia. He is a member of South Indiana Annual Conference of The United Methodist Church and has served pastorates in Indiana and Ohio.

Adrienne Carr is Professor Emerita of Christian Education at Candler School of Theology. She has served as Director of Children's Work and Director of Adult Education in churches in Colorado and Ohio.

John and Adrienne are experienced group leaders and also the authors of *Experiment in Practical Christianity, The Power and Light Company,* and *Prepare Ye.*

Mr. and Mrs. Carr have three sons and nine grandchildren.